The Jewish Domination of Hollywood

Peter Anderson

ISBN: 978-1500153342

© Peter Anderson

Contents

1. Preface   5
2. Introduction   6
3. Pre-Second World War: the 1920s   6
4. Pre-Second World War:
   the Challenges of the 1930s   11
5. Hollywood in the McCarthy Period   15
6. Hollywood in the late 20th Century and Early 21st Century:
   the Zenith of Jewish Power   19
7. Hollywood Now   20
8. References   21

Appendix One: Leading Jewish Film Executives   23

Appendix Two: Notable Jewish Film Directors   25

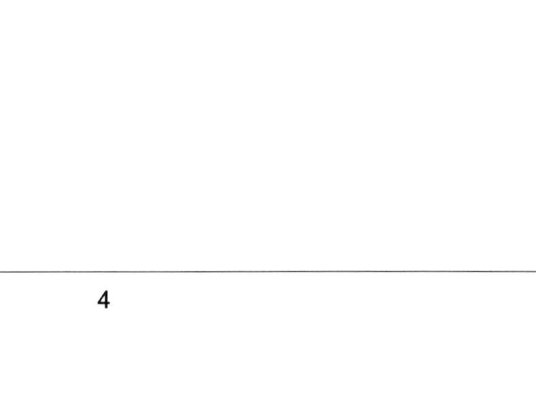

Preface

In her slightly light-hearted article in the British newspaper *The Guardian*, Lisa Marks (2008), asserts that "this is a great time to be a Jew in Hollywood" and she notes that "all eight major film studios are run by men who [are] Jewish". Marks herself is Jewish, but grew up in England, and she claims that in England she was less aware of her Jewishness, because it was simply ignored. However, she states that in Hollywood being Jewish is "one of the best calling cards in town". She ends her article with this observation:

> We've come a long way from the days when Tony Curtis felt the need to distance himself from the young Bernard Schwartz, or when Kirk Douglas was forced to ditch the cumbersome moniker, Issur Danielovitch Demsky, in his quest for fame.

If Gabler's general thesis in his book *An Empire of Their Own: How the Jews Invented Hollywood* is correct, then in one sense it has always been a great time to be a Jew in Hollywood, but, as this paper will demonstrate, the history of Jewish involvement in the movie business has been problematic, largely because of anti-Semitism and the exclusion of Jews from mainstream American life. At least we have reached a point in history where Jewish actors no longer feel the need to disguise their Jewishness by changing their name, as the examples of Ashton Kutcher and Mayim Bialik prove.

As this paper will show, the Jews involved in Hollywood have survived various difficulties and yet have survived to dominate the movie business. Appendix A (Jewish producers) and Appendix B (Jewish film directors), while not comprehensive, are still an impressive list of talent, and demonstrate the extraordinary influence that Jewish men and women have had in both the production and direction of many of the greatest films ever made in Hollywood.

Introduction

It may come as a surprise to some to discover that the first motion picture films were not made in Hollywood – they were made, usually in large cities, and predominately in New York. In addition, the earliest American films did not involve Jews at all. Thomas Edison invented the first camera that could record moving pictures and his agents enforced his ownership of the patent diligently. Rogin (1996) describes *Birth of a Nation* (1915) as "the single most important movie ever made" (p. 14). But it was made without any significant Jewish involvement and it was shot in Los Angeles. The content of the film was highly controversial, because it presented the Ku Klux Klan in a very positive light, and it was criticized heavily for this political and racist stance. However, cinematically and aesthetically, it was the first film to use techniques that would become a standard way of creating cinematic narrative. Techniques such as panoramic long shots, panning shots, flash-backs, the use of the iris lens, and the utilization of a tiny number of extras, shot to appear as if there were thousands of them were first used in Griffiths' film. In addition, gentiles the cameras, the lighting equipment, the projection achines, the raw film stock were all invented by gentiles. Even before *Birth of a Nation* (1915), Edwin S. Porter (a gentile) had made the first Western movie and the first films to present a narrative (Wikoff, 1989, p. 243). It is interesting to note that despite the overt racist content of *Birth of a Nation*, Louis B. Mayer bought the distribution rights.

Neal Gabler's book – *An Empire of Their Own: How the Jews Invented Hollywood* (2010) – uses the place name 'Hollywood' with knowing precision. Jewish producers, directors and actors played little part in the early beginnings of American cinema, but they did 'invent' or create the movie business in Hollywood, as we shall see. (Having said that, it was a group of English émigrés who set up the first film production company in Hollywood – the Nestor Studio in 1910.) But is certainly true that Jews came to dominate the movie business. This paper explores how they did it, why they did it, and the problems they encountered.

Pre-Second World War: the 1920s

The group of young Jewish men who set up most of the Hollywood studios in the early 1920s were united and similar in various ways They had a shared background: they were the sons of impoverished Jews from Eastern Europe; they had all grown up in New York's Lower East Side; they were ambitious for financial success and for assimilation into American society. Yet as Bernadi (2012) points outs, they were "marginal in American society because of their Jewishness" (p. 6). They had all been tangentially involved in the entertainment industry in New York and New Jersey before making the move to the West Coast: they all ran nickelodeons – small theatres were people paid a nickel to watch a silent movie.

Their reasons for moving to Hollywood were largely practical: labor was less organized than on the East Coast, so costs could be kept down; the weather allowed filming for longer during the day; they were geographically distant from the watchful enforcers of the Edison Patents Company; and the state of California offered a very wide variety of landscapes to film in. Did these Jewish studio founders engage in shady dealing? The answer is an emphatic "Yes". They used stolen Edison cameras to shoot their early movies and paid Edison no fees for their use (Wickoff, 1989, p. 242). Mayer falsified his bookkeeping so that Griffiths did not receive all the money he was owed for the distribution rights of *Birth of a Nation*: Mayer made $500,000 from that single film (Wickoff, ibid.). Ostracized and discriminated against by the anti-Semitic American mainstream, Wickoff (1989) suggests that the Jewish studio heads sought financing from Jewish organized crime or legitimate finance from banks owned by Italian-Americans who were, like the Jews, barred from certain high-earning professions by their ethnicity (p. 247). The studio heads also used contacts in the garment industry (dominated by Jews) to provide the costumes they needed (Bernadi, p. 5)

The Jewish heads of the major studios – "Jesse Lasky, Carl Laemmle, Adolph Zukor, Willian Fox, Samuel Goldwyn, Marus Loew, Louis B. Mayer, Irving Thalber, the Warner Brothers, Harry Cohn, Joe and Nick Schenk, David O. Selznick" (Rogin, 1996, p. 78) – were united also in what Bernadi (1996) calls their "non-Jewish Jewishness" (p. 7). [Rogin also points out that "of the major powers that dominated industry from the 1920s through to the end of the 1940s, only Cecil B. DeMille and Darryl Zanuck were not Jewish (p. 78).]

Gabler asserts that these men, so desperate were they to be accepted as Americans, became secular Jews: they did not keep kosher kitchens or eat kosher food; they did not attend synagogue. However, this overt rejection of their religion did not mean that they ever lost their sense of being outsiders or that they lost their keen sense of their Jewish cultural tradition. Hollywood musicals could be said to show continuity with the fine singing traditions of Russian and Yiddish singing, which by the 1920s was beginning to influence Broadway as well (Bulhe, 2009, p. 57). However, Hollywood films were also deeply rooted in American popular culture: Tin Pan Alley and vaudeville, which performers who were Jewish had started to dominate too (Rogin, 1996, p. 16). Even Yiddish theatre survived until the late 1920s, but faded because the younger generations of Jews were (like their counterparts in Hollywood) so determined to assimilate and to be accepted as Americans (Bulhe, 2009, p. 62).

Gabler (1988) claims that for the heads of the studios "Hollywood was a means of avoiding Judaism, not celebrating it" (p. 300). He claims that Hollywood was "founded and run for thirty years by Eastern European Jews who themselves seemed to be anything but the quintessence of America" and that they made films which were successful because "above all, they wanted to be regarded as Americans, not Jews; they wanted to reinvent themselves here as new men" (p. 34). Starting in the 1920s and continuing, it could be argued, to the present day, the Jewish-run Hollywood studios, gave America through their movies a vision of America: it gave Americans what they wanted to see. Gabler (1988) argues that the Jewish studio heads "colonized the American imagination" and that "the movies were quintessentially American while the men who made them were not" (p. 98).

The Hollywood moguls were from poor Jewish families who had emigrated at the end of the 19th century or the very beginning of the 20th century. It is worth pointing out that events in Europe – the Russian Revolution, Hitler's rise to power, the end of the Second World War – all lead to smaller waves of Jewish emigration to the United States. In these smaller waves of emigration "some of the finest actors, directors and designers who trained in Moscow and Berlin made their way" to America (Buhle, 2009, p. 62) and many of them were Jewish. Thus the pool of Jewish talent in acting, singing and directing was constantly being augmented and refreshed, which led to a further strengthening of Jewish power and control in Hollywood.

It is also wise at this point to remember the extent of anti-Jewish sentiment in America in the 1920s and beyond. Jews were not allowed to enrol at élite public schools or universities; they were barred from joining golf clubs and country clubs; American banks were reluctant to lend Jews money. Many of these bans continued into well into the 1960s, depending on the state. In Hollywood the Jewish studio heads reacted by opening their own country club – the Hillcrest Country Club. Even the name suggests their desire to be assimilated into a country that was, by and large, hostile to them.

The rampant anti-Jewish sentiments of most Americans led actors and actresses to change their Jewish names to names that sounded more solidly Anglo-Saxon, as this paper pointed out in the Preface above. Buhle (2009) asserts that "from the early sound films until the 1950s a remarkable pretence or convention remained formally intact… [seen in] the altered names of so many Jews in acting, writing and production" (p. 51). Bernadi (2012) argues that the experience of being

Jewish – not being accepted in society and, in Eastern Europe, over the course of centuries, being the victims of violence and real, physical hatred – gave Jewish writers and actors a general empathy for all oppressed or downtrodden people anywhere in the world, a natural sympathy for the underdog, we might say. Bernadi (2012) goes even further by claiming that Jewish actors and actresses "could draw on Jewish experiences in forming their screen personae and creating characters that endeared them to the box office. Yet moviegoers were not always aware that Jewish experience was unfolding in front of their eyes" (p. 6).

This section will end with a discussion of the famous Al Jolson film, *The Jazz Singer* (1927), because, for a wide variety of reasons, it is a seminal, landmark film in the history and development of Hollywood. Simply in terms of cinema history, *The Jazz Singer* was a technical breakthrough and a commercial success: Rogin (1996) claims that "*The Jazz Singer* broke all previous box office records" (p. 15). In cinematic terms, *The Jazz Singer* was a hugely important innovation: the first musical movie in the world. It is even more remarkable in its content, because it presents the dilemma of being Jewish in a mainstream film: audiences would have to wait until *Exodus* (1960) for another film in which the Jewish experience was so clearly central to the plot. The plot of *The Jazz Singer* involves a Jewish character whose chance for success in American society is challenged by his Judaism: his opening night on Broadway clashes with his promise to sing at his local synagogue. The film resolves the issue by delaying his opening night, so that he can fulfil his obligations to his faith by singing at synagogue AND also have success on Broadway, in mainstream American culture. Al Jolson's character symbolizes the aspirations of the Jews who ran Hollywood – they wanted to do justice to their religious backgrounds, but also achieve success in America. What is even more interesting is that Jolson on Broadway sings in black-face, a common habit at the time: white singers would 'black up' to resemble African-American minstrels. Of course, we now find such a practice unimaginably crass and offensive. However, Jolson's use of black-face is an apt symbol for the dilemma of Jews in America. They were not discriminated because of color; they had no problem as 'passing' for white – indeed, they were white, but they still faced prejudice and discrimination. Therefore, *The Jazz Singer* presents one despised racial minority disguising itself as another despised racial minority in order to gain success in white, Christian America. Rogin (1996) argues that Jews were more sensitive and sympathetic to the problems of African-Americans, because they suffered the same discrimination and, because African-Americans rarely appeared in films in that era, "Jews could speak for blacks but not blacks for Jews" (p. 17).

The profits from *The Jazz Singer* allowed Warner Brothers to buy their own chain of movie theaters in urban America, a trend that had begun 1924 and had been started by M.G.M. This increased Hollywood's financial hegemony: they made the films, distributed them and showed them. By the end of the 1920s all the major studios owned their own chain of urban movie theaters.

Pre-Second World War: the Challenges of the 1930s

On the surface, in the 1930s Hollywood and its Jewish moguls enjoyed continued commercial success of its films and the continued profits the Hollywood studios made (largely because of a more organized system of overseas distribution which opened mass markets in Great Britain and Germany, thus increasing a film's potential profits). However, there were tensions in the industry, caused largely by external factors over which the film industry had little control. Firstly, the Depression went on throughout the decade; secondly, the Hays Code was rigorously enforced, causing constant disputes with movie makers; and, thirdly, the rise of Hitler in Germany and his anti-Semitic policies caused problems in faraway Los Angeles. Buhle (2009) describes the studio bosses as "captains of industry in a one industry town, the moguls thus presented models of assimilation…upset only by the Depression and the rise of Fascism" (p. 65).

In fact, the Hays Code was the least of their problems. It was a code designed to regulate taboo language, nudity, sexual content and racial mixing – as presented in Hollywood films. It was vigorously supported by the Catholic Church and by extreme Protestant churches, and acted as a moral censor of the content of Hollywood films.

The Depression was a difficulty because high unemployment could affect box office figures. The other problem was how the studios reacted to the country's economic plight: were films to reflect the harsh realities of the Depression or were they to offer entertainment to distract a population burdened by falling living standards and less disposable income? There was a political side to this. Roosevelt was first elected as president in 1933 and introduced a series of economic reforms which came to be known as the New Deal. Republican critics of Roosevelt saw in the New Deal a socialist program of reform and accused him of being in league with Moscow; popularly and unfairly, the New Deal was given the derogatory title of the Jew Deal. (Doherty, 2013, 46). Doherty also claims that the 1930s were "boom times for ant-Semitism" (p. 53) and, therefore, the studio heads were wary of films that were too political in content or too supportive of the New Deal – they did not want to inflame American anti-Semitism. It was not until 1940, after the outbreak of war in Europe, that the film version of *The Grapes of Wrath* was released. The film is strongly supportive of the New Deal and champions socialist values.

The election of Hitler in 1933 and his implementation of vigorous anti-Jewish policies exacerbated the situation. Doherty points out that German-Americans distributed anti-Semitic propaganda written by Goebbels, and, in terms of the plots of Hollywood films, after 1934 there was Doherty (2013) "the exclusion of high-profile Jews after 1934" (p. 54). Fox had two films banned in Germany – *My Weakness* and *Country Doctor*, the latter because the Nazi regime assumed that the actress Jean Hersholt was Jewish. Fox Studios (because of the financial importance of the new German market) went to great lengths to prove that she was "untainted by Jewish blood" (Doherty, 2013, p.

196) but the ban remained in force. Hitler even appointed an envoy to Hollywood (George Gyssling) to liaise with the studios, so that they avoided subjects such as the Nazi treatment of the Jews and also to ensure that Germany and Germans were presented in a very positive light. This had a real effect on the films that were made. Some scripts were turned down because of the desire to appease the Nazis. A script called *The Mad Dog of Europe* was written which was explicitly about the destruction of a Jewish family in Nazi Germany (Quinn, 2013,). The German watchdog, Gyssling, approached the Hays Office (which enforced the Hays Code) and Joseph Breen, the head of the Code in L. A., turned the script down. He wrote to Herman J. Mankiewicz, the author of the script:

> Because of the large number of Jews active in the motion picture industry in this country, the charge is certain to be made that the Jews, as a class, are behind an anti-Hitler picture and using the entertainment screen for its own propaganda purposes. (Quinn, 2013)

The project was abandoned. Another example is that of a novel by Sinclair Lewis, entitled *It Can't Happen Here*. The novel is set in the future and portrays the rise to power in America of a fascist dictator. Louis B. Mayer was very keen to turn the novel into a film, Hollywood's first anti-fascist movie. MGM even purchased the film rights. Breen urged Mayer not to make the film, arguing that it would be "dangerous" and "inflammatory" (Quinn, 2013). Mayer ignored this advice and work started on the film. However, the Chairman of the Film Committee of the Central Conference of American Rabbis wrote to Mayer: "The only wise method to pursue in these days of virulent anti-Semitism is to have no picture in which the Jewish Problem is ventilated" (Quinn, 2013). The film was abandoned.

What may seem pusillanimous on the part of Hollywood is, in fact, no different from the policy of appeasing Hitler which the western democracies followed before the outbreak of World War Two. The Hollywood moguls acted as they did because, firstly, they wanted the box office receipts from German film audiences, and, secondly, they also wanted to avoid stirring up anti-Jewish feeling in America. Schindler (2005) argues the studio heads knew "there was a deep, not so latent anti-Semitism in America, and memories of the pogroms they had experienced in Eastern Europe had never disappeared (p. 64). And so they continued to make films that Middle America liked, not just for the money, but from a deep desire to be assimilated and a naïve belief in the American Dream. Schindler expresses their motives like this: "it wasn't just that the film's chances of success would be enhanced if they were liked by Middle America, the moguls believed passionately in the fantasy of goodwill to be found behind the white picket fences of America" (p. 57). But some films celebrating liberal values were made in the 1930s. Finkelstein (2002) argues that the Jews of Hollywood "transformed their Jewish back rounds into films containing universal themes" (p. 84). The best example of this is the film *They Won't Forget* (1937) which was based on a true story known as the Leo Frank case. Leo Frank was a Jew living in the Deep South who was brutally and illegally lynched by Southern racists in 1913. He was the manager of a factory in Georgia who was accused of the murder of a young girl who worked at the factory. The evidence was circumstantial, but Frank was convicted of the crime and imprisoned. Later a mob of local citizens, including well-known local businessmen and politicians, kidnapped him from jail and carried out the lynching. The film itself follows the Leo Frank story very accurately – except that the 'Leo Frank' character is not Jewish: the film presents him as a liberal Yankee from the north. Once again we see the trend to present a story about injustice (akin to the injustice of anti-Semitism), but disguised in order not to aggravate anti-Jewish feeling in America.

Despite the conflicts and problems, Hollywood ended the 1930s on a high with the release in December 1939 of *Gone with the Wind* – a film that is now regarded as one of the finest ever made. When one factors in changes in inflation and the value of money, *Gone with the Wind* is far and away the biggest grossing film in the history of Hollywood and the world. It is also often credited as being the first film ever to present black characters in a sympathetic, non-stereotypical way. Financially the 1930s were good for Hollywood: by concentrating on films that were instantly recognizable to the movie-going public and were clearly identifiable as belonging to a certain genre – Westerns, biopics, historical epics, comedies, lavish musicals, animated cartoons – they catered to the public's taste. MGM also singlehandedly pioneered the star system which encouraged loyalty to a particular actor or actress – and the studio that employed them, since the stars were kept on salary by individual studios. Studios also began to have certain values associated with them: MGM had the most famous stars; Warner Brothers films seem to have been the most liberal and radical: not only had they produced *The Jazz Singer* (discussed above) but the two Hollywood films banned by the Nazis were products of the Warner Brothers studio.

Hollywood in the McCarthy Period

The mid-1940s were Hollywood's heyday: in 1946 Hollywood produced over 400 films which were watched by 96 million Americans (Gabler, 1988, p. 276). The Second World War was over and Hitler's fascist, racist regime had been overthrown by America and its allies – which would eventually give rise to another popular genre: the war movie. In contrast to the anti-Semitism of the past, the public knowledge and awareness of the Holocaust had resulted, according to Buhle (2009) in "public guilt about the Holocaust" and there arrived in Hollywood a "new wave of actors and director from Germany – Fritz Lang, Billy Wilder, Michael Curtiz, Otto Preminger and Fred Zinnemann" (p.175). The American economy was growing again and was to usher in a new era of prosperity. All seemed perfect for Hollywood to consolidate its past successes and continue to make commercial and artistically memorable films.

However, three developments, in very different ways, were to force Hollywood to change its ways and threatened its hegemony in the entertainment business. Firstly, television, a new medium, took audiences away from the cinema and changed Hollywood artistically: Hollywood was forced to make a different type of film. Secondly, the major studios lost the rights to distribute their own films and to own the movie theaters. Thirdly, and more sinisterly, the Cold War and the witch-hunt led by Senator Joe McCarthy threatened at best unemployment and at worst prison for those involved in the entertainment industry who held, or who had once held, socialist or communist beliefs.

Hollywood met the challenge of television by making films that could not be made by the television studios, because they lacked the financial muscle or the technical know-how. Therefore, Hollywood released fewer films each year, but those films had far bigger budgets as they sought to utilize more lavish sets, unusual outdoor locations and more and more sophisticated special effects – the very things that early television could not compete with.

In 1938 the first attempts were made to challenge the major studios monopoly control of the films, their distribution and their showing in studio-owned theaters. The challenge was based on anti-trust legislation brought in the Roosevelt government, essentially as a move to remove monopoly control of any industry and open them up to others for wider business opportunities. The Second World War delayed the case, as well as the major studios own defensive legal appeal, but after the war the case was settled and the studios had to sell the distribution rights and they also had to give up ownership of all the movie theaters they had acquired. This led to the break-up of the studio system and, in a sense, the star system: studios no longer kept stars or directors and their creative teams on contract. Paradoxically this drove up wages in the industry, since star actors and directors could drive up their fees, and this links with the point above about fewer films being made, but with significantly larger budgets than in the past. The age of the Hollywood blockbuster was in its infant stages.

The immediate post-war mood in Hollywood was very positive. The victory over fascism and Hitler's racist regime meant that "after the war, Hollywood made several films about anti-Semitism and race" (Fried, 1990, p. 78). In the light of the coming Cold War and the red witch-hunt led by Senator McCarthy, the film *Days of Glory* (1944) is an astonishing film, in retrospect. It is a significant film anyway because it marked the screen debut of Gregory Peck. In 1944 the Soviet Union was an ally of America, and the film presents a group of Soviet partisans, fighting the Nazis behind the front line, in a wholly positive light. It is a film that could not have been made at any other moment of history, and could not have been made in 1948, for example, a mere four years later. Fried (1990) also notes that "after 1947 the number of message films declined" (p. 78).

The Cold War changed everything. Fearing the widespread dissemination of socialist and communist beliefs in all aspects of American life, the House UnAmerican Activities Committee was set up – to identify those Americans who had or once had socialist or communist sympathies. The classic question that they posed was, "Are you now or have you ever been a member of the Communist Party of America?" Those who co-operated with the committee – by confessing and by naming the names of others they had seen at left wing meetings - were let off lightly. Those who refused to co-operate were blacklisted and could not work in their profession, or in extreme cases, they were sent to prison. The HUAC investigated all levels of American society and all professions: however, the world of Hollywood and, to a lesser extent, the academic world of the universities were investigated disproportionately – because these walks of life included many Jews with left wing ideals or beliefs. A group known as the Hollywood Ten protested about HUAC's activities, arguing that the committee's actions broke the First Amendment – the right to complete freedom of speech. The group consisted of a mixture of Jewish actors and directors. However, HUAC dealt harshly with the Ten, and the studios agreed to blacklist those who fell foul of the committee. Litvak (2009) asserts that HUAC had a huge impact on the "Jewish world of show business" (p. 5) and that by "keeping the blacklist to keep in with the true wielders of power, Hollywood sought to dissociate itself from Jewish intellectualism" (p. 16). In an attempt to ingratiate themselves with HUAC, the studios made many anti-communist films, but, Fried (2009) notes "none were distinguished or remarkable" (p. 40). Apart from their political beliefs, Jewish actors were still wary of inflaming anti-Semitism and this was still an era when they chose to change their names. However, in the eyes of HUAC this made things worse: Buhle comments 52 "they were essentially parading under Gentile labels, a practice…considered prima facie evidence of their Un-American intentions" (p. 52). The 1976 film The Front is interesting in this context. It deals with the subject of black-listing and the majority of the people who worked on the film had been blacklisted in the 1950s. Indeed, the final credits follow each individual's name with the year that they were blacklisted: all levels of the movie industry were effected – directors, actors, even camera operators and sound recordists.

    However, HUAC's influence gradually diminished as the 1950s went on and the 1960s began with a triumph for Hollywood: the release of the film *Exodus*, which deals with the formation of the state of Israel and was produced and directed by Otto Preminger, a leading Jewish director.

    Another very positive event took place in 1952 – although its impact was not seen immediately. The Hays Code still restricted or censored American films, but the Supreme Court ruled that movies were works of art and should enjoy the protection of the First Amendment – freedom of speech. This paved the way for more sexually adventurous films in the 1960s and the rating system. Hollywood films could no longer by censored by a government agency.

Hollywood in the Late 20th Century and Early 21st Century: the Zenith of Jewish Power

In the 1960s American domestic life was dominated by two major issues: the fight for Civil Rights by African-Americans and the domestic opposition to the Vietnam War. In addition, in retrospect, we can see that the decade also saw the beginnings of the counter-cultural revolution – which encompassed the struggle for Civil Rights and opposition to the war, but involved a much wider range of lifestyle choices and attitudes – generally more liberal and tolerant. The end of the decade also saw the beginnings of feminism and the Gay Pride movement.

All these phenomena were to be reflected eventually in Hollywood films, but they had a much more important impact: being Jewish began to matter less and less. As Carr (2001) puts it attitudes changed and anti-Semitism decreased as the general population realized that "Hollywood Jews were neither the subversive Communists nor the greedy capitalists that had appeared in so much anti-Semitica of yore" (p. 2). Jewish actors no longer felt the need to change their names and in *Raiders of the Lost Ark* (1981), Steven Spielberg felt able to utilize two vital Jewish obsessions in an essentially light-hearted adventure movie. Jewish obsession with the scared importance of the Lost Ark of the Covenant is central to the film's plot, and the Nazis are almost cartoon-like baddies. Spielberg followed this in 1993 with *Schindler's List* – one of the most-watched films in the history of cinema and widely acknowledged as one of the best films ever made. Critics had felt that a serious film about the Holocaust could not be successful, but, and this may seem a trite way to express it, *Schindler's List* and changing social attitudes made it almost unfashionable to be anti-Semitic.

Hollywood Now

The Preface to this essay began by referring to Lisa Marks' 2008 article in *The Guardian*. In her article she mentions the *L. A. Times* journalist, Joel Stein, who reported the findings of a poll by the Anti-Defamation League which, in 2008, found that only 22% of Americans believe that Hollywood is run by Jews. By contrast, in 1964, the League found that 50% of Americans thought that the Jews ran Hollywood. This tells us more about public perceptions than reality. Marks asserts that the movie business and the television industry is still dominated by Jews: in each industry about two-thirds of its participants are Jewish – from the owners to the directors to the actors to the armies of technical staff.

The Anti-Defamation League's polling might tell us something more: that public attitudes have changed and that the general public no longer 'see' being Jewish as very important. It seems, perhaps, to have become a non-issue.

Hollywood and its Jews have survived the Hays Code, the lobbying of the Nazis, HUAC, the advent of television and the arrival of VHS and DVDs. More importantly, they have survived and seemed to have conquered anti-Semitism. Some of their survival has been due to appeasement and compromise, but their main goal has remained the same: to bring good movies to the world. In that sense, their story is one of unparalleled success.

References

Aitken, Harry & Griffiths, D. W. (Producers). Griffiths, D. W. (Director). (1915). *Birth of a Nation*. Epoch Producing Company.

Bernadi, Daniel. (2012). *Hollywood's Chosen People: The Jewish Experience in American Culture.*

Buhle, Paul. (2009). *From the Lower East Side to Hollywood: Jews in American Popular Culture.*

Carr, Steven Alan. (2001). *Hollywood and Anti-Semitism: A Cultural History Up to World War II.*

DeSylva, Buddy G. (Producer). Butler, David. (Director). (1933). *My Weakness*. Fox Film Corporation.

Doherty, Thomas Patrick. (2013). *Hollywood's Code: Joseph Breen and the Production Code Administration.*

Finkelstein, Norman H. (2002). *Forged in Freedom: Shaping the Jewish-American Experience.*

Fried, Richard M. (1990). *Nightmare in Red: The McCarthy Era in Perspective.*

Gabler, Neal. (2010). *An Empire of Their Own: How the Jews Invented Hollywood.*

Joffe, Charle H. & Ritt, Martin. (Producers). Ritt, Martin. (Director). (1976). *The Front*. Columbia Pictures.

Litvak, Joseph. (2009). *The Un-Americans: Jews, the Blacklist and Stoolpigeon Culture.*

Marks, Lisa. (24 December 2008). Why it's still great to be Jewish in Hollywood. *The Guardian.*

Quinn, Anthony. (16 October 2013). The Collaboration: Hollywood's Pact with Hitler. *The Guardian.*

Marshall, Frank (Producer). Steven Spielberg (Director). (1981). *The Raiders of the Lost Ark*. Paramount Pictures.

Preminger, Otto. (Producer and Director). (1960). *Exodus*. Universal Artists and MGM.

Robinson, Casey. (Producer). Tourner, Jacques. (Director). (1944). *Glory Days*. RKO Radio Pictures.

Rogin, Michael. (1996). *Blackface, White Noise: Jewish Immigrants in the Hollywood Melting Pot.*

Schindler, Colin. (2005). *Hollywood in Crisis: Cinema and American Society 1929 – 1939.*

Selznick, David O. (Producer). Fleming, Victor. (Director). (1939). *Gone with the Wind*. Selznick International Pictures & MGM.

Spielberg, Steven. (Producer and Director). (1993). *Schindler's List*. Universal Pictures.

Warner, Jack. (Producer). Crosland, Alan. (Director). (1927). *The Jazz Singer*. Warner Brothers.

Warner, Jack. (Producer). King, Henry. (Director). (1936). *Country Doctor*. Warner Brothers.

Warner, Jack. (Producer). Leroy, Mervyn. (Director). (1937). *They Won't Forget*. Warner Brothers.

Wickoff, Jack. (1989). Review of *An Empire of Their Own: How the Jews Invented Hollywood*. *The Journal of Historical Review*, Summer 1989, Volume 9. No. 2, pages 243 -246.

Zanuck, Darryl F. & Johnson Nunnally. (Producers). Ford, John. (Director). (1940). *The Grapes of Wrath*. Fox Film Corporation.

Appendix One

Leading Jewish Film Executives

Leading Hollywood movie moguls and pioneers of the studio system era were Jewish: Louis B. Mayer and Samuel Goldwyn (Metro-Goldwyn Mayer MGM) William Fox (Twentieth Century Fox), Jesse L. Lasky and Adolph Zukor (Paramount Pictures), Harry Cohn (Columbia Pictures) and Marcus Loew (Loews Pictures), Harry, Albert, Sam, and Jack Warner (Warner Brothers) and Carl Laemmle the founder of Universal Studios.

Other less famous Jewish executives were/are:

Barney Balaban was president of Paramount Pictures from 1936 to 1964, and innovator in the cinema industry.

Charles O. Baumann was an American film producer, film studio executive, and a pioneer in the motion picture industry.

Michael Dammann Eisner is an American businessman. He was the chief executive officer of The Walt Disney Company from 1984 until 2005.

William Fox was a pioneering American motion picture executive, who founded the Fox Film Corporation in 1915 and the Fox West Coast Theatres chain in the 1920s.

David Geffen is an American business magnate, producer, film studio executive and philanthropist. Geffen was also one of the three founders of DreamWorks SKG in 1994.

William Goetz was an American Hollywood film producer and studio executive.

Gary Goetzman is an American film studio executive, film and television producer.

Samuel Goldwyn was an American film producer. He was most well known for being the founding contributor and executive of several motion picture studios in Hollywood.

Brad Grey is the chairman and CEO of Paramount Pictures, a position he has held since 2005.

Peter Guber is an American film producer and executive and chairman and CEO of Mandalay Entertainment. Films he personally produced or executive produced include Rain Man, Batman.

Nina Jacobson is an American film executive who, until July 2006, was president of the Buena Vista Motion Pictures Group, a subsidiary of The Walt Disney Company.

Jeffrey Katzenberg is an American businessman, film studio executive and film producer. As a businessman, he is the CEO of DreamWorks Animation and is also known for his tenure as chairman of The Walt Disney Studios from 1984 to 1994

Carl Laemmle in Los Angeles, California) was a pioneer in American film making and a founder of one of the original major Hollywood movie studios – Universal.

Sherry Lansing is an American former actress and film studio executive. She is a former CEO of Paramount Pictures, and when she was the president of production at 20th Century Fox, she was the first woman to head a Hollywood studio

Jesse L. Lasky was an American pioneer motion picture producer.

Al Lichtman was a businessman working in the motion picture industry. He also occasionally worked as a film producer. Lichtman has a "Star" on the Hollywood Walk of Fame.

Marcus Loew was an American business magnate and a pioneer of the motion picture industry who formed Loews Theatres and Metro-Goldwyn-Mayer (MGM).

Siegmund Lubin was a German-American motion picture pioneer.

Louis Burt Mayer was an American film producer. He is generally cited as the creator of the "star system" within Metro-Goldwyn-Mayer (MGM) in its golden years. He was one of the founders of AMPAS famous for its "Oscars" Academy Award.

Larry Meistrich is an award-winning film producer. He was a founding member of the now defunct film production company The Shooting Gallery.

Ron Meyer is an American entertainment executive and former talent agent.

David V. Picker is a motion picture executive and producer, working in the film industry for more than forty years. He has served as President and Chief Executive Officer for United Artists, Paramount, Lorimar and Columbia Pictures.

Rich Ross is Chief Executive Officer for Shine America, responsible for commercial strategy of the Shine Group in the United States. He had previously been the president of entertainment at Disney Channel, and chairman of Walt Disney Studios.

Mo Rothman was a Canadian-born, American studio executive who persuaded Charlie Chaplin to return to the United States in 1972, ending Chaplin's twenty year, self-imposed exile.

Dore Schary was an American motion picture director, writer, and producer, and playwright who became head of production at Metro-Goldwyn-Mayer and eventually president of the studio.

Joseph M. Schenck was an American film executive. He played a key role in the development of the American film industry.

Nicholas Schenck was an American film studio executive and businessman.

David O. Selznick was an American film producer and film studio executive. He is best known for producing *Gone with the Wind* (1939) and *Rebecca* (1940), both earning him an Academy Award for Best Picture, and *The Third Man* (1949).

Appendix B: Notable Jewish Film Directors

[Dates given indicate year of birth]

1 Alan Arkin 1934

2 Alan J. Pakula 1928

3 Amy Heckerling 1954

4 Anatole Litvak 1902

5 Barry Levinson 1942

6 Barry Sonnenfeld 1953

7 Bennett Miller 1966

8 Billy Wilder 1906

9 Brett Ratner 1969

10 Bryan Singer 1965

11 Carl Foreman 1914

12 Carl Reiner 1922

13 Cecil B. DeMille 1881

14 Chris Weitz 1969

15 Christopher Guest 1948

16 Darren Aronofsky 1969

17 David Zucker 1947

18 Don Siegel 1912

19 Douglas Fairbanks 1883

20 Edward Bernds 1905

21 Edward Zwick 1952

22 Ernst Lubitsch 1892

23 Ethan Coen 1957

24 Fred Zinnemann 1907

25 George Axelrod 1922

26 George Cukor 1899

27 Harmony Korine 1973

28 Harold Ramis 1944

29 Herbert Ross 1927

30 Irvin Kershner 1923

31 Irwin Winkler 1931

32 J.J. Abrams 1966

33 Jack Arnold 1916

34 James L. Brooks 1940

35 Jay Roach 1957

36 Jerry Lewis 1926

37 Joel Coen 1954

38 Joel Schumacher 1939

39 John Landis 1950

40 Joseph L. Mankiewicz 1909

41 Judd Apatow 1967

42 Lawrence Kasdan 1949

43 Leonard Nimoy 1931

44 Lewis Milestone 1895

45 Mel Brooks 1926

46 Michael Curtiz 1886

47 Michael Mann 1943

48 Mike Nichols 1931

49 Miloš Forman

50 Nora Ephron 1941

51 Norman Lear 1922

52 Oliver Stone 1946

53 Otto Preminger 1905

54 Peter Bogdanovich 1939

55 Richard Benjamin 1938

56 Richard Brooks 1912

57 Richard Fleischer 1916

58 Rob Cohen 1949

59 Rob Reiner 1947

60 Robert Rossen 1908

61 Robert Wise 1914

62 Sam Mendes 1965

63 Sam Newfield 1899

64 Sam Raimi 1959

65 Samuel Fuller 1912

66 Sidney Lumet 1924

67 Spike Jonze 1969

68 Stanley Donen 1924

69 Stanley Kramer 1913

70 Stanley Kubrick 1928

71 Steven Spielberg 1946

72 Susan Seidelman 1952

73 Sydney Pollack 1934

74 Todd Haynes 1961

75 Tony Kaye 1952

76 William Friedkin 1935

77 William Wyler 1902

78 Woody Allen 1935

79 Zach Braff 1975

80 Zalman King 1942

Printed in Great Britain
by Amazon